Dawn of Happiness

By:

Sitora Pardabayeva

ISBN 978-93-5872-135-5

Book	:	Dawn of Happiness
Author	:	Sitora Pardabayeva
Publisher	:	Taemeer Publications
Year	:	'2023
Pages	:	38
Title Design	:	*Taemeer Web Design*

Development of carpet making in Uzbekistan

An Uzbek household cannot be imagined without a carpet. Carpet making has developed in our country since ancient times as a form of artistic craftsmanship. So what do we know about its history? In which regions of our carpet is it woven? What raw materials were used to weave it?

According to historical data, carpets were used in palaces and rich households, and palos, felt (felt) and olacha, bald carpets were used in middle-class families. The nomadic tribes engaged in animal husbandry also used them in the grasslands. Firstly, the sheep wool used for the carpet was warm, and secondly, insects did not get close to it. The ground inside the grassland was covered with a carpet or a reed mat made of felt. along with preventing rotting, it ensured the durability of the carpet (because if it was laid directly, it could rot or mold). Even before the khans began to rule the state, they were transferred to white felt and raised to the top. By this, they put forward the belief that their king rose as high as the sky and became equal to God.

To give another example, Farhod Eshmo'minov describes the surprise of the Spanish ambassador Claviho Amur when he came to the Temur palace in his work "Fountains of Aksaray" and quotes the following sentences: So, the carpet was used not only for the needs of ordinary people, but it had a special place in events and gatherings of state importance. That's why carpet weavers and craftsmen are valued and praised.

Carpet-making has long been developed among the nomads who made a living from animal husbandry, and later settled people engaged in agriculture. It is difficult to say when the carpet appeared. The oldest carpets were found in the mountainous Altai region, dating back to the 5th-6th centuries BC.

The carpets of the peoples of Central Asia are distinguished by the clarity and beauty of the patterns, the symbolism of every detail in the decorations, and the harmony of colors.

The color of the carpets is red, and because they worshiped fire according to the beliefs of patriarchy, they considered its color sacred. Blue, black, yellow, and white colors were considered secondary colors. White was distinguished by purity, innocence, and the color of the sky. Craftsmen combined each color with mastery and skill, thereby achieving color and attractiveness. Carpets are made of cotton, It is woven from flax fiber and goat, sheep, camel hair. For this purpose, sheared wool is washed and cleaned, combed with iron combs. has not changed and has not lost its quality.

Carpets are woven on special looms. In some places, due to the perfection of the looms, several weavers could sit side by side and weave one carpet. Each detail in the decoration is distinguished from each other by the location of the patterns and has its own symbol. For example, the "lock-key" symbol of the olacha carpet means that the doors of the houses are open for friends and closed for enemies.

According to the method of weaving, carpets are divided into types with or without feathers. There are traditional styles of Bukhara, Sahrisabz, Urgut, Nurota, Bulung'ur and other regions in weaving carpets without feathers.

Karakalpakstan, Khorezm, and Jizzah regions also have their own characteristics of carpet weaving.

Surkhan carpet weavers are famous for their bald carpets. They reflect the religious ideas and beliefs of our people. Weaving carpet is a difficult process. 12-14kg is used for one carpet.

A felt is also a floor or grass made of wool, a covering for the house. To prepare it, it is crushed, ground and ground using a wooden stick. After the threads are colored, they are placed on the edge, and various flowers and signs are printed on them. Basically, it is decorated with rhombus and cross-shaped patterns. After that, a little water is sprinkled on it and it is wrapped around one edge. After several repetitions, the product is ready.

In the mountain villages of Sanam, Ovjazsoy in Ohangaron district of Toskent region, traditions of carpet weaving and felting have been preserved. Local residents have been teaching the secrets of this ancient craft to their children and students.

During the former Soviet period, factories producing carpets were built in Uzbekistan, and their products were delivered to neighboring republics, and carpet weaving rose from a home craft to an industrial level. After independence, modern techniques and technology entered the carpet industry, and Uzbek carpets found their place in the world market. Today, carpets produced in our country have reached the level of quality and competition from the leading carpet manufacturers of Turkey, Belgium, and Iran.

Carpet making, which is a unique type of folk arts and crafts, among the immortal traditions and values of our people, has reached us over the centuries, and will be inherited and developed by the future generations, acquiring a new spirit and modernity.

***

Young talents

Sitora Pardabayeva, a student of the field of study "Repair of works of art" of the National Institute of Painting and Design named after Kamoliddin Behzod under the Academy of Arts of Uzbekistan, Faculty of Applied Arts, was awarded the "O' "Education in Uzbekistan" magazine was awarded with the "Talent" badge.

***

Sitora Pardabayeva, a 3rd-level student of the Faculty of Applied Arts at the National Institute of Painting and Design named after Kamoliddin Behzod, has her first solo exhibition of tapestry and other types of applied art, "Happiness was organized under the name of "Epkins".

More than 30 creative works of the artist were included in the exhibition, including composite tapestries of different content and examples of decorative applied art.

METHODS OF DRAWING GEOMETRIC PATTERNS USING COMPUTER GRAPHICS IN APPLIED DECORATIVE ARTS

NAMansurov - associate professor of MRDI named after Kamoliddin Behzod,

S. Pardaboeva - 3rd grade student

The policy of the Republic of Uzbekistan in the field of education, universal human values, historical experience of the people, centuries-old traditions in the field of culture and science, taking into account the future development of the society, is carried out. Including, great work is being done in the education system. State standards, programs, textbooks in each field have been redeveloped and are being further improved. World science, science and technology fields are developing very fast, new researches and productions are growing every minute. In particular, in continuous education, public education workers and professors in higher and secondary special vocational schools and academic lyceums face enormous tasks.

Currently, computer graphics are widely used not only by academics, but also by artists, designers, design and advertising professionals, web site creators, teaching process and other fields. Therefore, one of the tasks before us is to train mature personnel in the field of computer graphics, to deliver computer graphics literature to young readers.

One of the computer graphics programs is CorelDRAW. The CorelDRAW document file format is CDR. The CDR file format is a vector image or graphic image created with CorelDRAW. This file format was developed for use in Corel, i.e. color maintenance products.

CorelDraw program is very wide, for example, let's look at the sequence of creating three different types of floral patterns. To create a form, we create a new page by selecting File > Create or Ctrl+N. Then we can draw a straight line by pressing the Dvukhtochechnaya line or F5 button on the toolbar. Draw another spiral shape around this straight line. This shape can be drawn as shown below by pressing the Spiral or A button on the toolbarz.

We draw a straight line by selecting the Peretekanie item from the Peretekanie section on the toolbar. Select the shape for coloring and right-click on the desired color from the Palette section. Select the form using the Instrumentov vybora command located on the toolbar, enter the number 70 in the Peretekanie obektov item located on the equipment bar, and select the Peretekanie po chasovoy strelke item located here. (Figure 2)

Also, geometric patterns in most types of folk decorative art

(girihs) are used and taught. But there is a dearth of resources for teachers and students about the origin and history of the girih pattern. Taking this into account, we would like to briefly touch on the history and origin of geometric patterns in applied art and architecture.

Geometric pattern, i.e. gyrix patterns, began to be used at the beginning of the 8th century. Girih flourished in the decorative arts of Central Asia and the Middle East in the 9th-12th centuries. For example, Varakhsha, Sugd fortress, Zarafshan valley, Khiva cities can be seen in architectural and practical art decorations, examples of ganch carving. Each of the geometrical patterns used as decoration, gihiras, is made based on certain laws.

Girix is a complex pattern with a strict pattern. The master can direct the varieties in any direction when drawing an Islamic copy. If you don't like it, you can turn it off and fill the empty spaces with flowers, buds or leaves. But when drawing a girikh pattern, the master is subject to the girikh he is drawing. Because each circle is created based on geometrical laws. Geometric patterns are very common in Central Asia and Middle Eastern countries.

Girih ornament flourished especially in the 9th-12th centuries. In architecture, the technologies of working on various bubble surfaces and embossing, i.e. kundal method, have been developed. Mathematician Abu al-Jurjani from Khurasan (940-998) in his book "What the Craftsman Needs from Geometric Shapes" was the first to create complex and simple geometric shapes using a ruler and a ruler.

459 showed ways to solve many problems of making forms. The correctness of geometric ornaments depends on the fact that its distribution is divided without remainder according to certain geometric features. These equal parts can be repeated in consonance or vice versa.

You will see that intricate decorations in the compositions of architecture and applied art are made in different ways. Countless giri patterns have been made based on the method of combining giri elements, complicating simple giri, dividing the giri into several parts, adding two giri divisions to each other.

The purpose of studying the types of girih in applied decorative arts:

- types of geometric pattern, its content, methods of creating geometric patterns in applied art,

introduce the requirements to them;

- materials and equipment used in creating geometric patterns, their use

training training;

- perfect various geometric pattern compositions from simple to complex

teaching to compose;

- painting, hanch carving, miniatures, material science and others for students

Consolidation of the knowledge acquired from the subjects, teaching to create a composition of geometric patterns on objects of different shapes, and at the same time focusing on the selection of colors to match.

- teaching the methods of creating a geometric pattern composition for voluminous items;

- teaching how to create various geometric pattern compositions for interior and exterior decoration;

- introduction to the beauty, philosophical, spiritual and educational aspects of Eastern applied art on the basis of composition classes.

Art historians such as B. Denike, L. Rempel, G. Pugachekova, G. Gaganov, B. Zasipkin, N. Baklanov, M. Bulatov, P. Zohidov, Z. Bositkhanov have studied the field of art. And our masters Shirin Murodov, A. Boltaev, M. Usmonov, J. Khakimov used them in their practical creations.

Zakirkhan Bositkhanov, Honorary Doctor of the Research Institute of Art Studies of the Academy of Arts of Uzbekistan, conducted serious scientific research with patterns related to gyrih. The master organized a personal exhibition in January 2001. More than 85 hilmahil girikh compositions from his exhibition left a great impression on art lovers. The master created about 400 girix samples. Especially, the master's book "Solution of Geometric Patterns" published in 2002 deserves praise in this regard. This manual is used by students and teachers in the study of examples of modern architecture and folk decorative art.

Now in our republic, talented masters of applied art Makhmud Usmanov, Makhmud Toraev, Anvar Ilhomov, Kamil Karimov, Hayotilla Abdullaev, Mansur Murodov and Khakimjon Inagamov, whose designs are used to decorate modern magnificent buildings, are characterized by their simplicity and beauty, the originality of the solution and distinguished by perfection.

It aims to deepen the installation of geometric patterns in applied decorative arts, and to carry out new scientific researches in theoretical and practical training. Printing of albums, methodical manuals, visual aids and training manuals for secondary vocational colleges, general education schools, additional educational institutions and higher education institutions, available makes it possible to solve problems positively.

References

1. Z. Bositkhanov. "Solution of geometrical patterns" - T.: Publishing house of art of Uzbekistan, 2002, - 38 p.

2. K. Gulomov. Artistic processing of objects. - T.: Knowledge, 2004, - 37 p.

3. T. Riksiboev. Computer graphics. - T.: Publisher of the Literary Fund of the Writers' Union of Uzbekistan, 2006, - 168 p.

4. Gary David Bouton. CorelDraw X7: The Official Guide. McGraw-Hill Education, New York, USA. 2015. – 705 p.

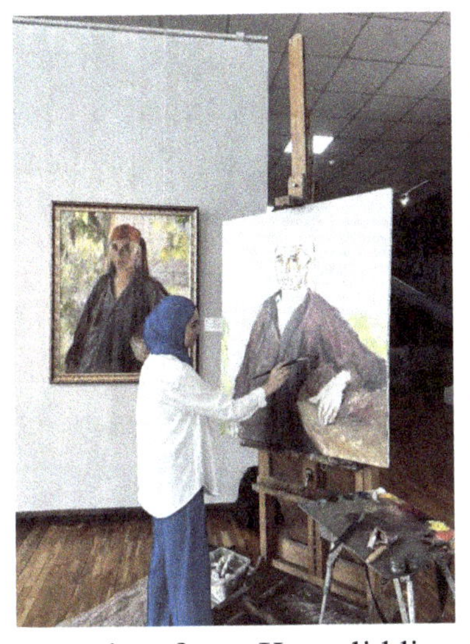

Pardaboeva Sitora Oybek kizi was born on April 30, 2002 in Piskent district of Tashkent region. He graduated from the Republican College of Design with an honors diploma in the specialty "Master artist designing carpets and tapestries". Currently, he is a 3rd-level student of the field of applied art restoration at the National Institute of Painting and Design Behzod, Faculty of Applied named after Kamoliddin Arts.Sitora Pardaboeva has been participating in several international contests and festivals, receiving diplomas, cups and medals. In particular, he is an active participant in a number of organizational events such as "Kamolot Cup", "Future Foundation of Ancestors' Heritage", "The Most Active Member of Kamalot".

"Clothes design" nomination at the district stage of the contest "Neighborhood - my destiny" under the motto "You are the cradle of values, my dear neighborhood", organized by the Piskent district branch of the "Mahalla" charity public fund, in order to create among young people historical memory, high spirituality, respect for the historical traditions and cultural heritage of the Uzbek people. won the 1st place and the proud 3rd place at the regional level.

He took part in the Republican contest "Yuksak navyatli avlod" and won the honorable 1st place, the 1st place in the district stage of the "Serkuyosh hur olkam" Republican competition, the proud 2nd place in the regional stage, and the proud 1st place in the "Talented Children's Conference".

It is the owner of the "Silver Medal" of the International Fine and Applied Arts Festival, which is traditionally organized annually by the Academy of Arts of Uzbekistan and the Association of Artists.

Sitora Pardaboeva has been taking pride of place not only in republican competitions, but also in international arenas. In particular, she is the grand prix winner at the "Art-nova" international festival held in St. Petersburg, Russia, and the 1st place laureate of the "Parad talantov Rossii" competition.

Sitora Pardaboeva, one of the young creators of tapestry art, has 30 creative works in her personal exhibition entitled "Bakht epkinlari", including tapestry works of various content and various types of applied art.

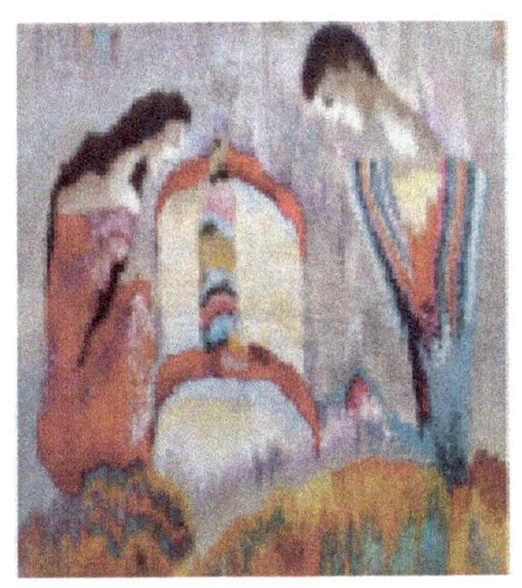

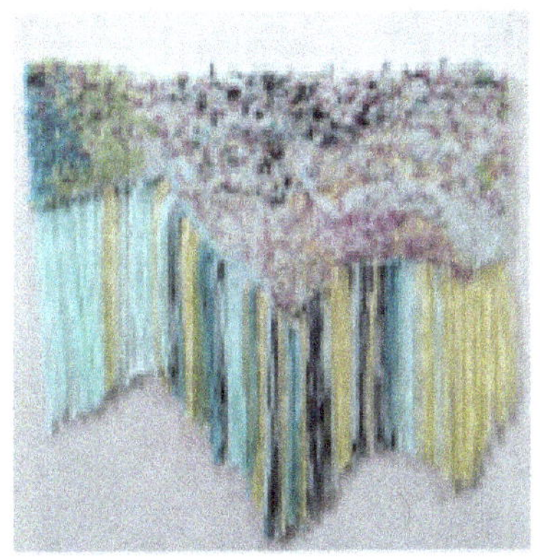

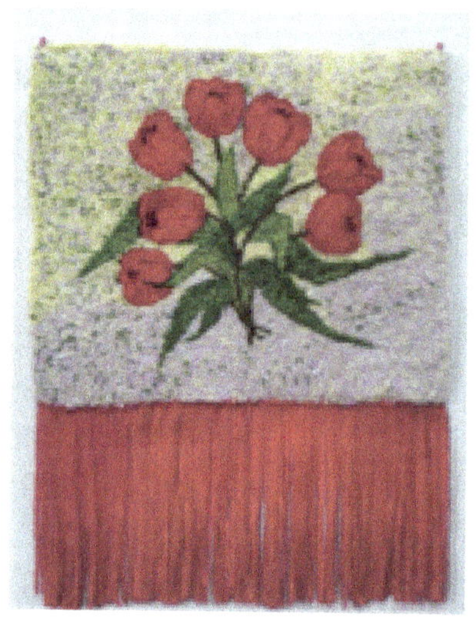

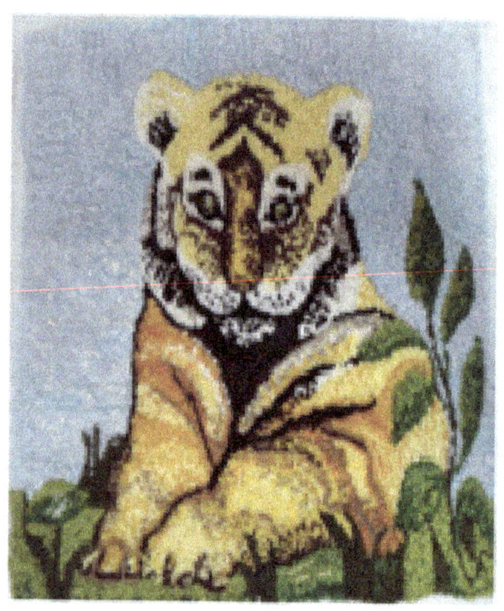

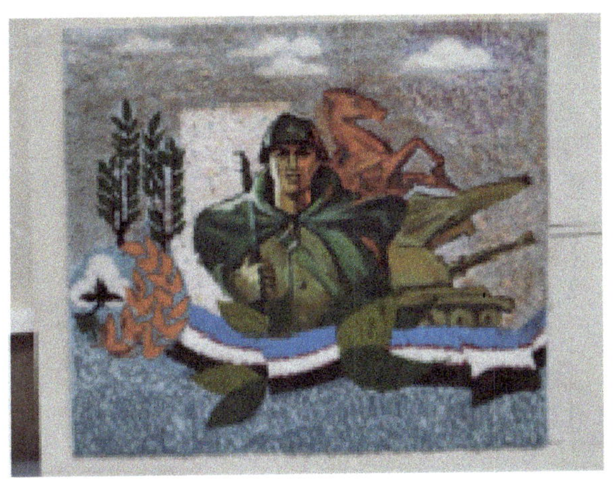

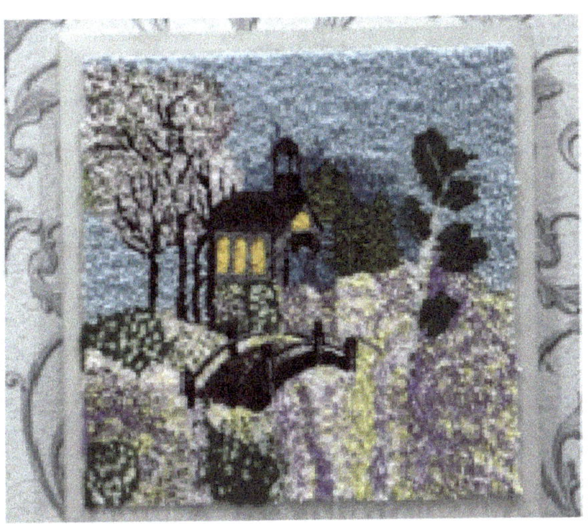

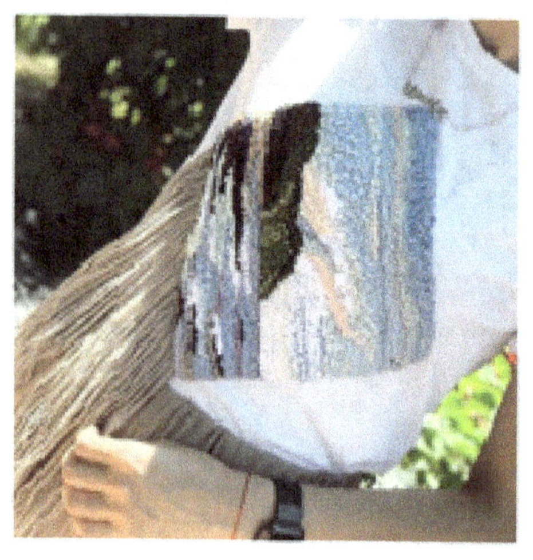

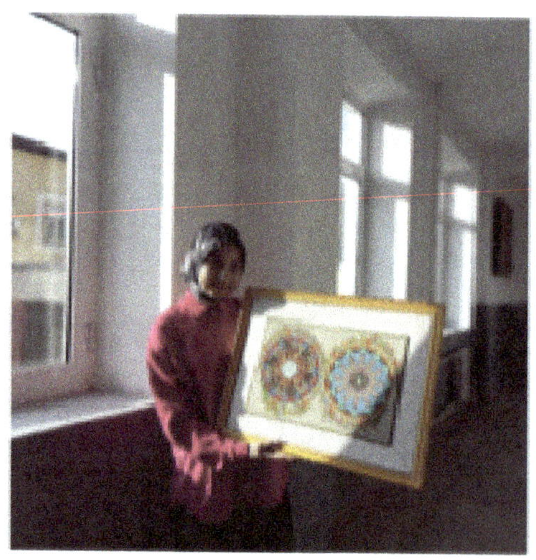

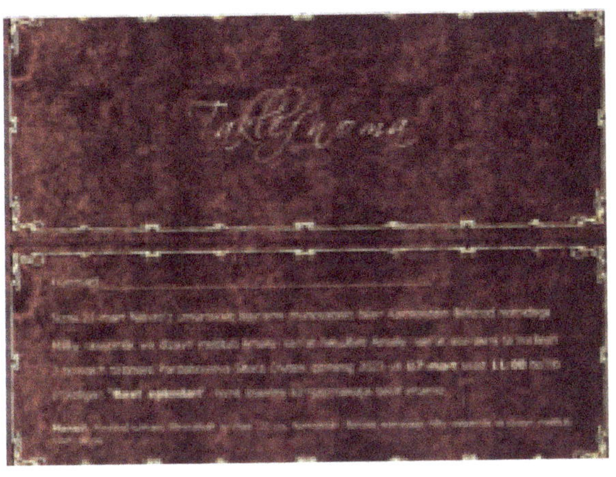

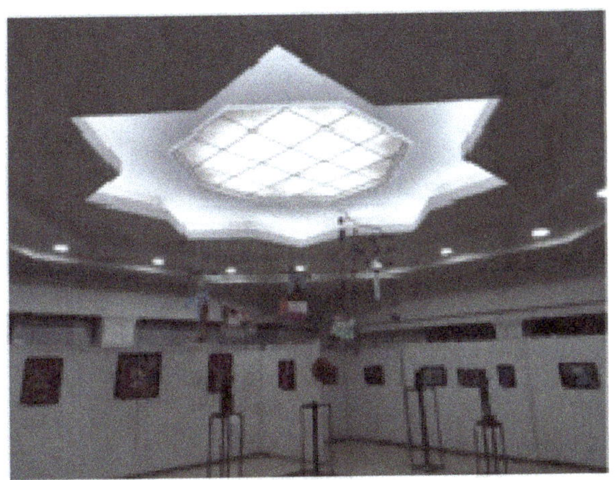

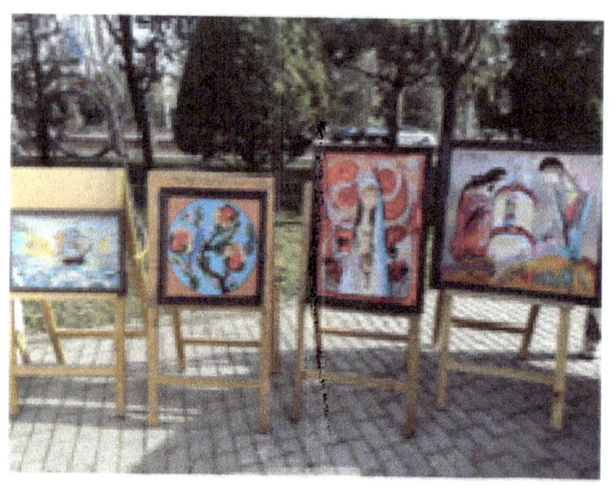

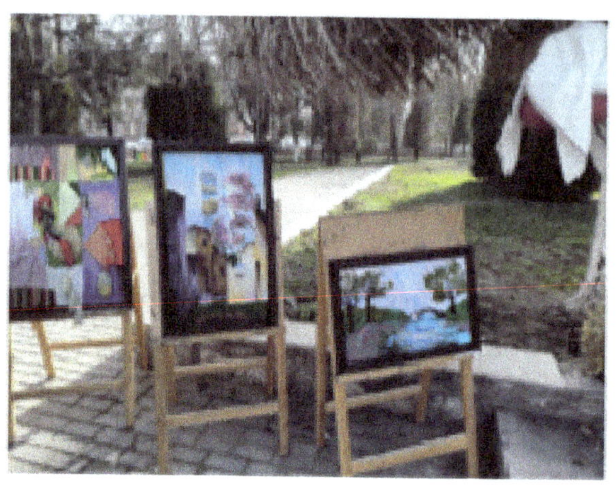

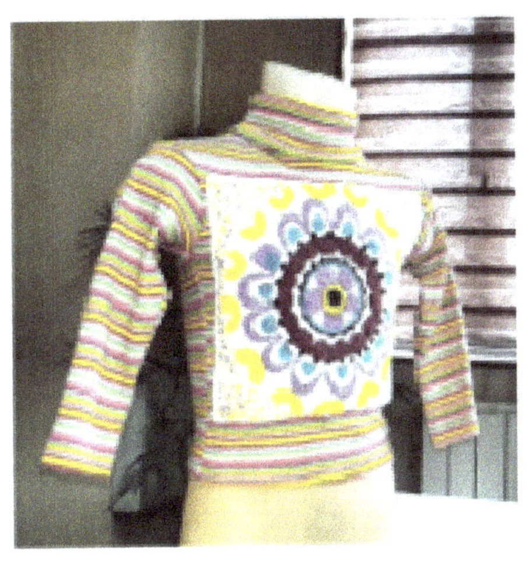

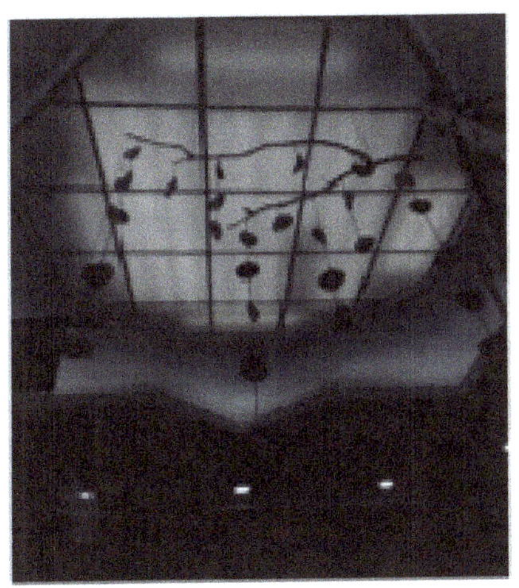

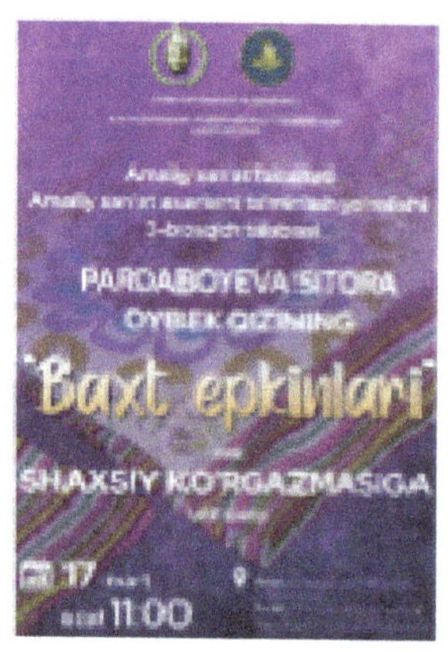

Amaliy san'at fakulteti
Amaliy san'at asarlarini tayyorlash yo'nalishi
3-bosqich talabasi
PARDABOYEVA SITORA
OYBEK QIZINING
"Baxt epkinlari"
SHAXSIY KO'RGAZMASIGA
17
11:00

Taklifnoma

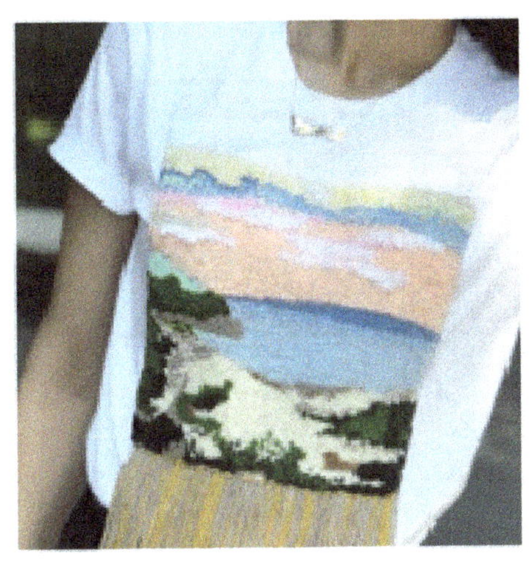

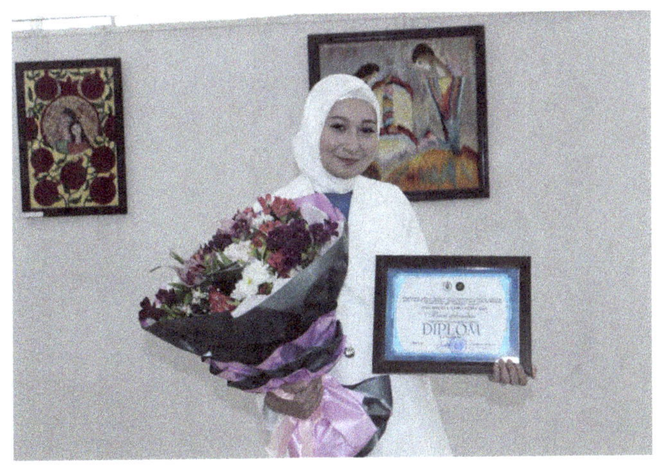

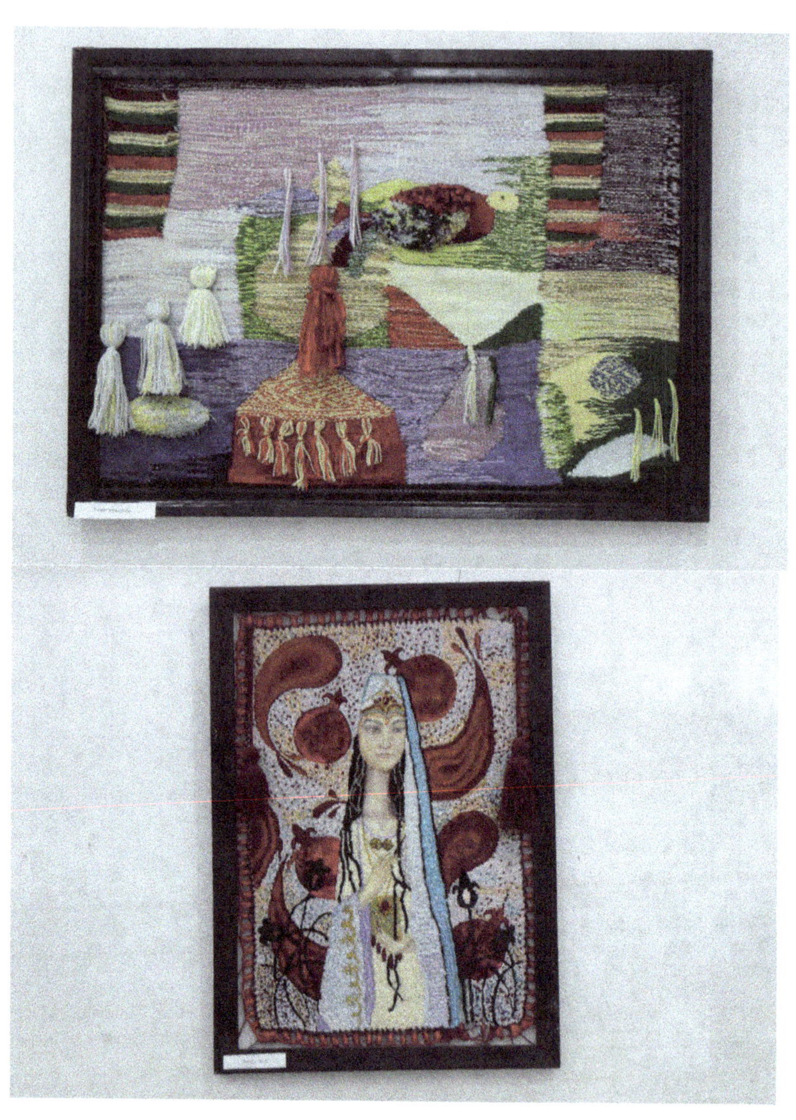

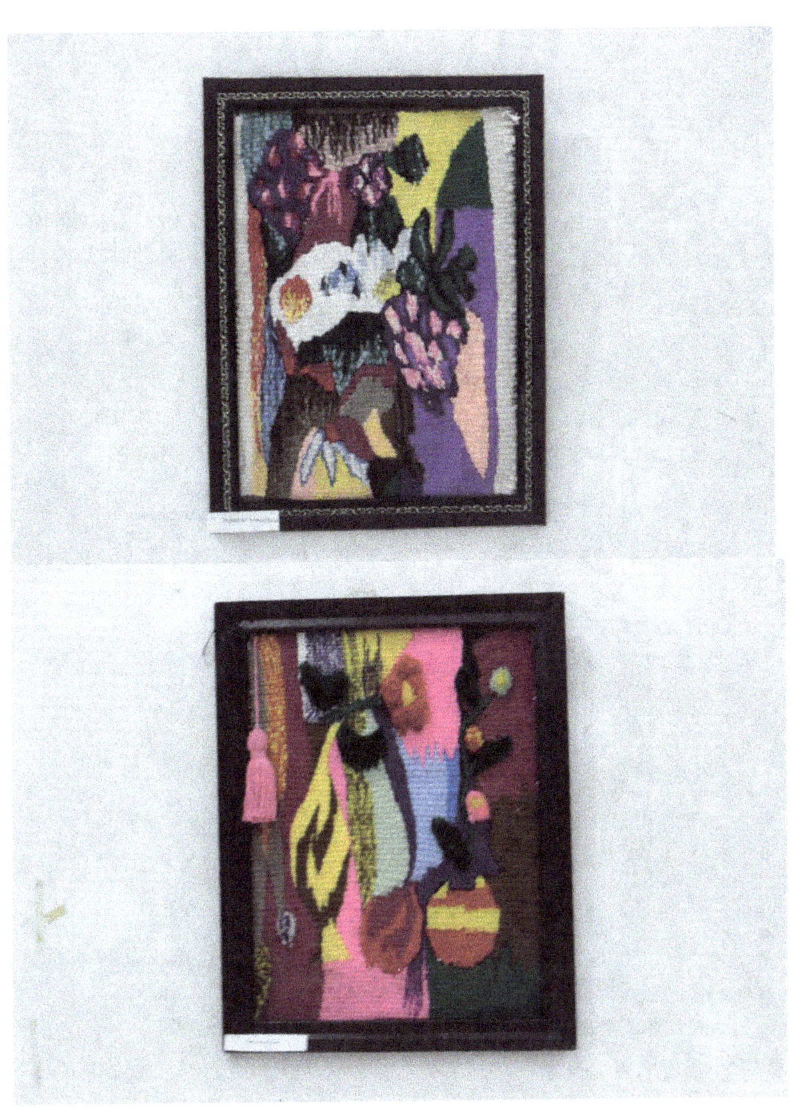

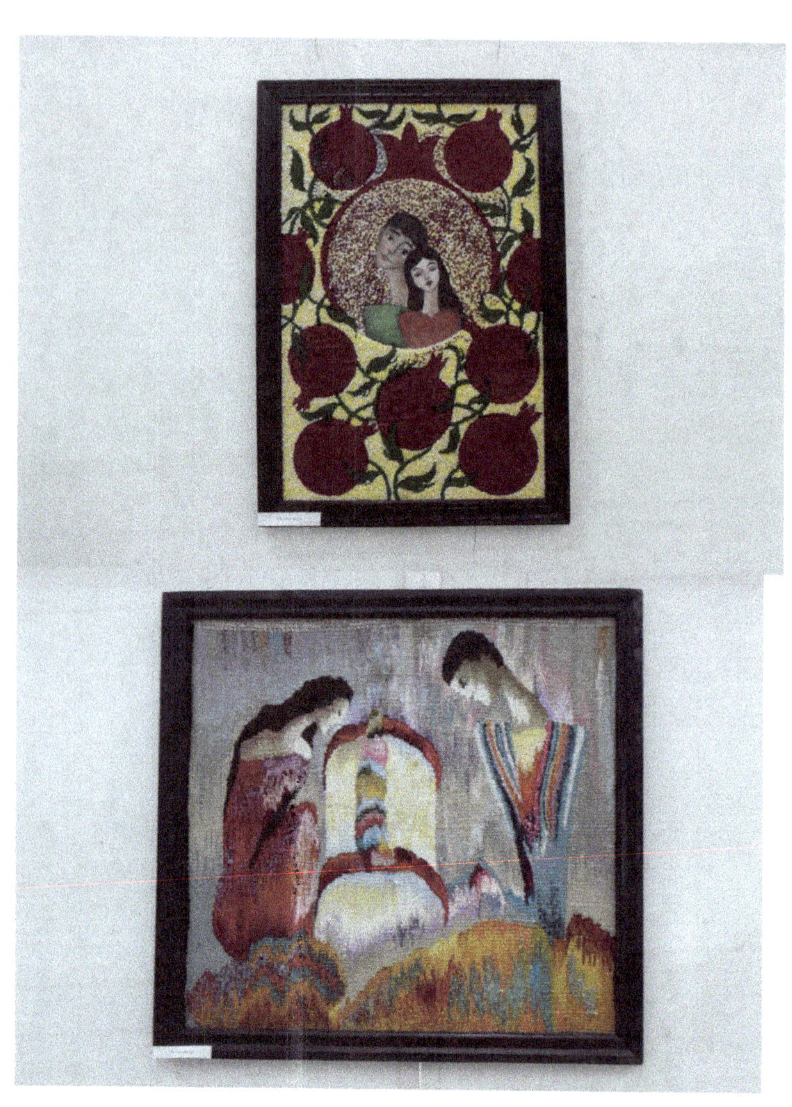

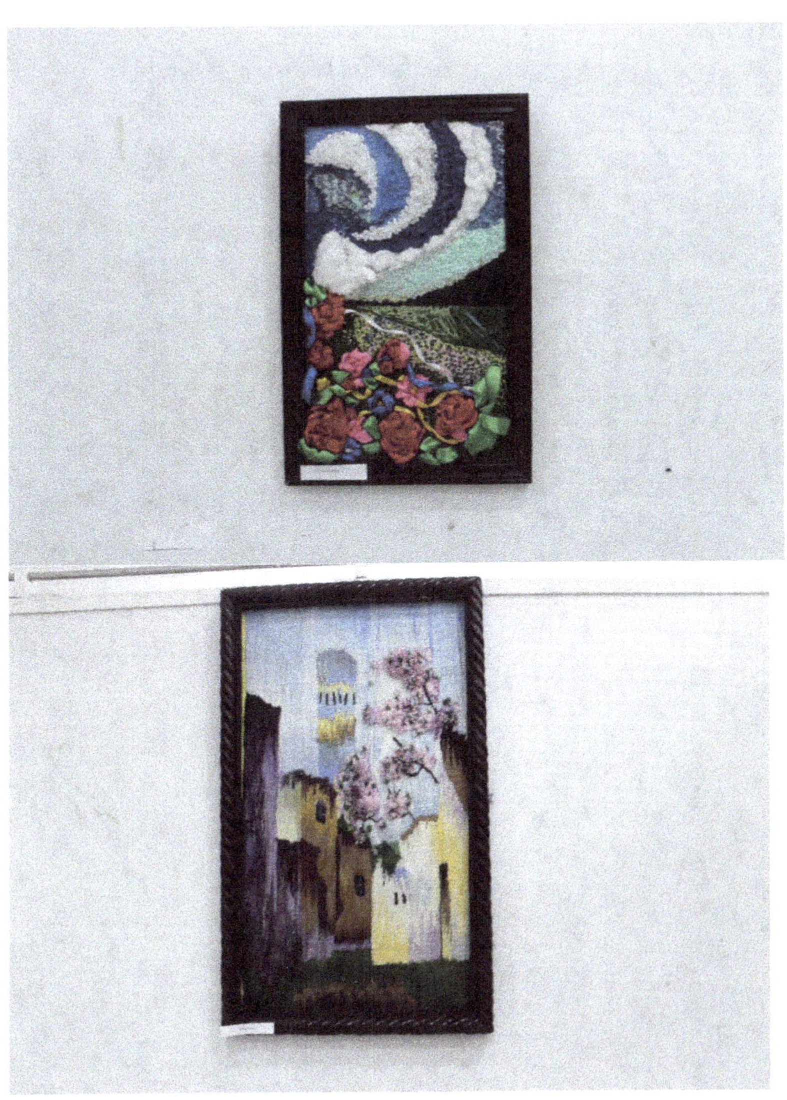

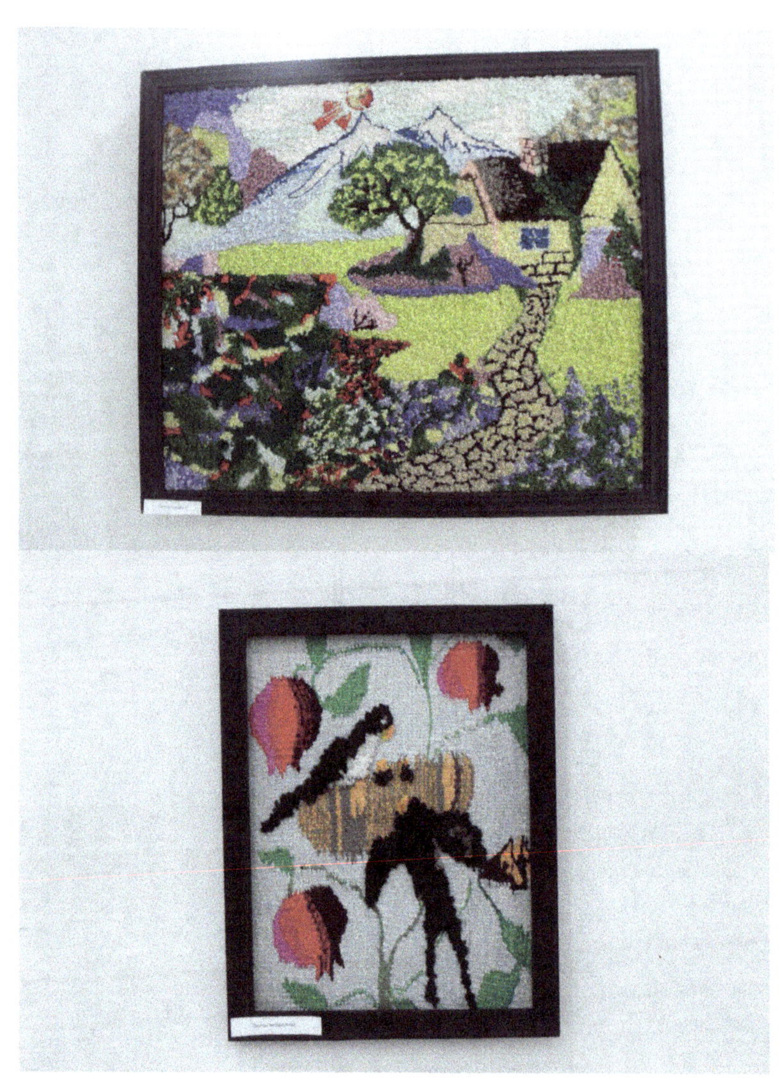

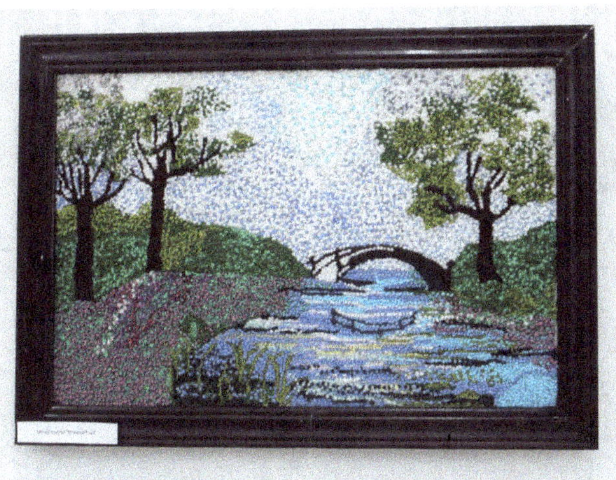

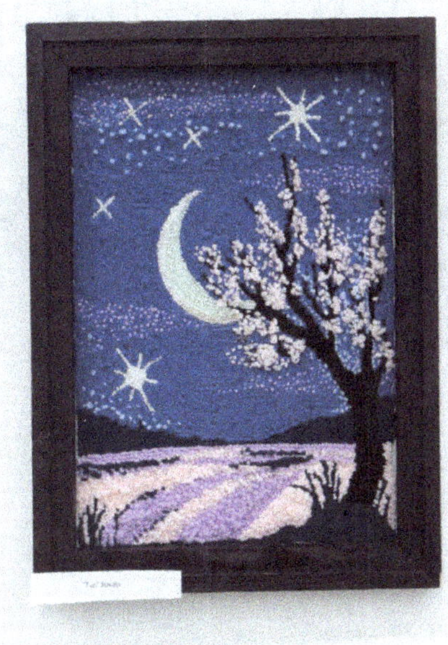

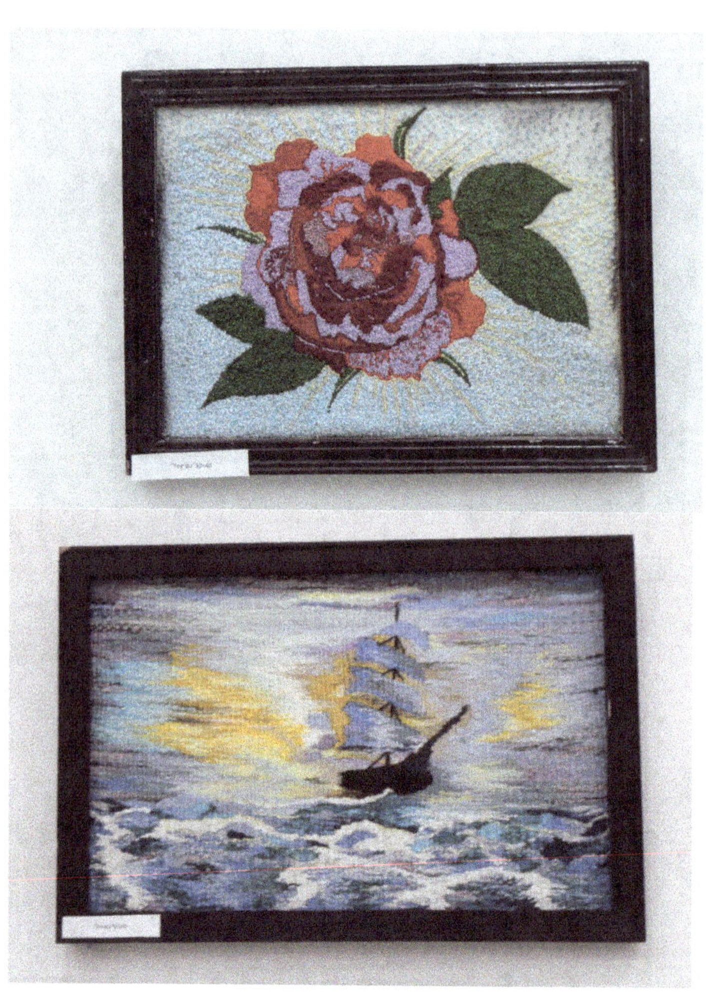

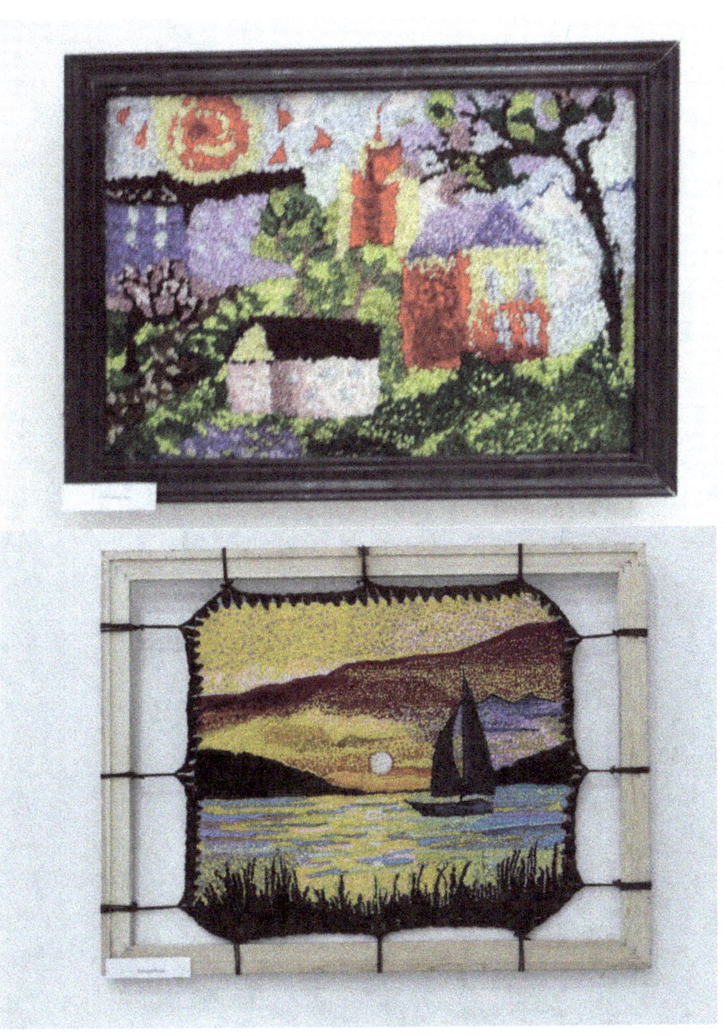

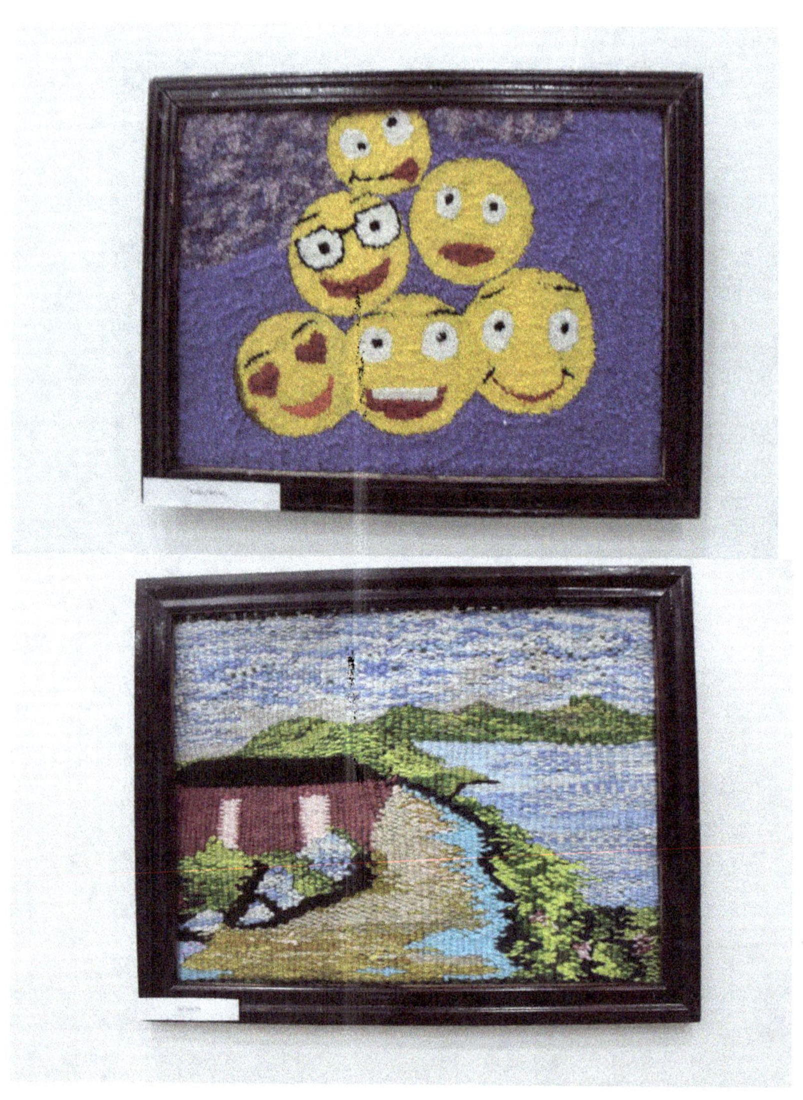

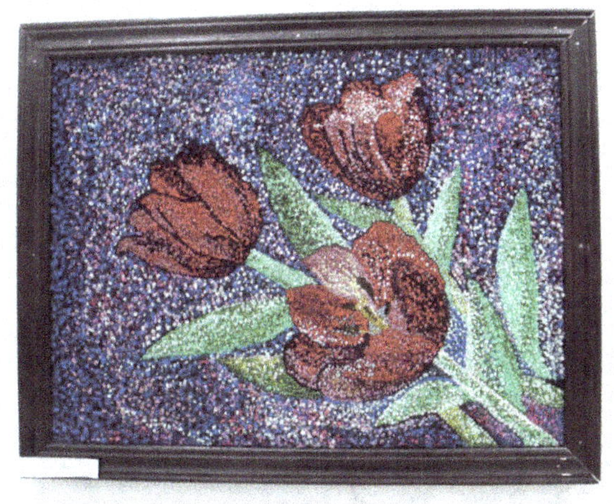

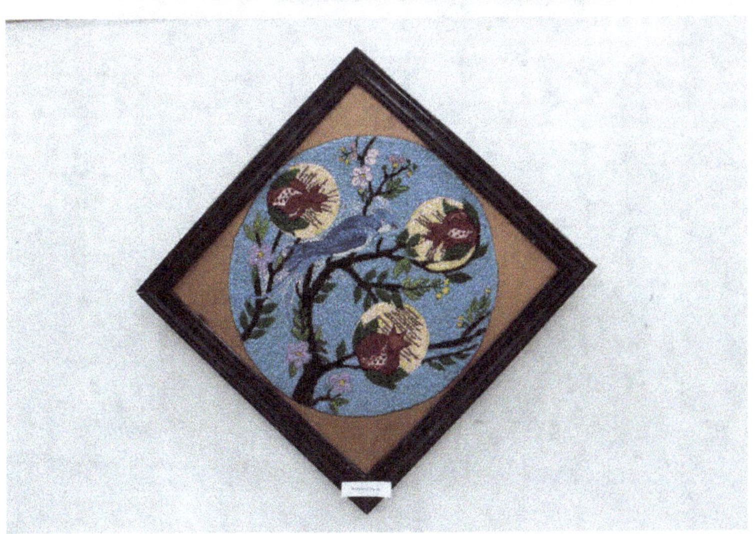

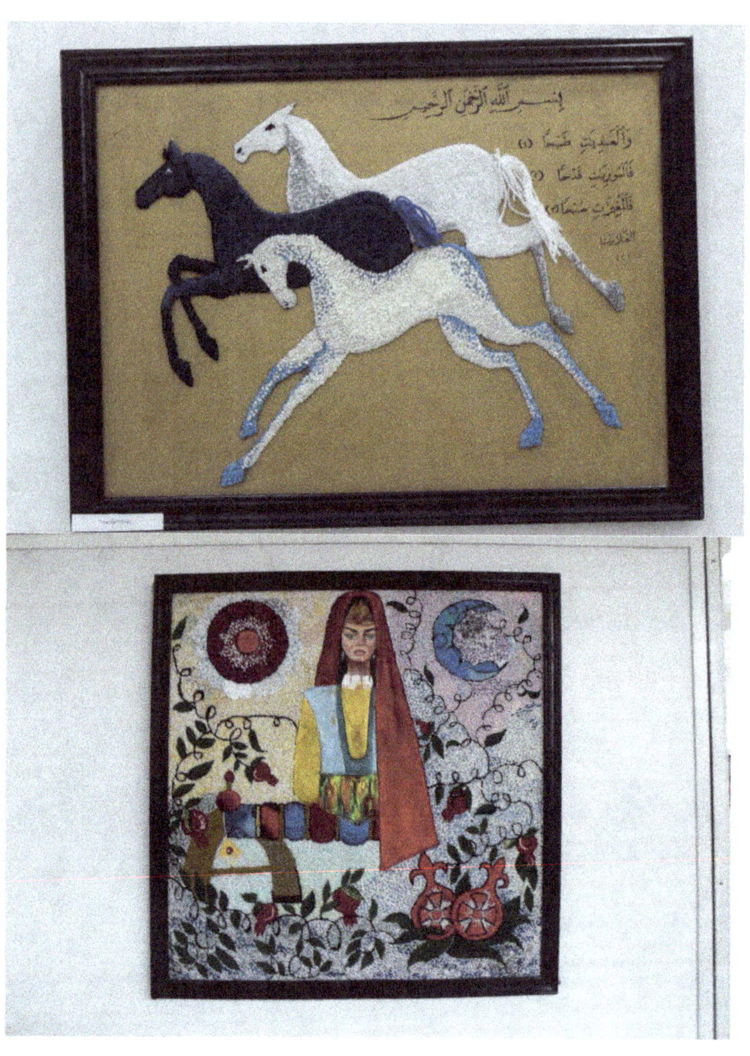